A-Z OF WELLBEING TOOLKIT

A mental health resource book for primary schools and churches

Ruth Rice and Debbie Green
Illustrated by Debbie Green

Authentic

Copyright © 2025 Ruth Rice and Debbie Green

First published 2025 by Authentic Media Limited,
PO Box 6326, Bletchley, Milton Keynes, MK1 9GG.
authenticmedia.co.uk

The right of Ruth Rice and Debbie Green to be identified as the Authors of this Work
has been asserted in accordance with the
Copyright, Designs and Patents Act 1988.

All rights reserved.
No part of this publication may be reproduced, stored
in a retrieval system, or transmitted in any form or by any means,
electronic, mechanical, photocopying, recording or otherwise, without
the prior permission of the publisher or a licence permitting restricted
copying. In the UK such licences are issued by the Copyright Licensing
Agency, 5th Floor, Shackleton House, 4 Battle Bridge Lane, London SE1 2HX.

British Library Cataloguing in Publication Data
A catalogue record for this book is available from the British Library.
ISBN: 978-1-78893-399-5
978-1-78893-400-8 (e-book)

Unless otherwise stated Scripture is taken from the International Children's Bible® (Anglicised Edition)
© 1991, 2005 by Thomas Nelson, Inc. All rights reserved.

Scripture quotations marked gnt are from the Good News Translation in Today's English
Version – Second Edition Copyright © 1992 by American Bible Society. Used by Permission.

Scripture quotations marked niv are taken from The Holy Bible, New International Version Anglicised
Copyright © 1979, 1984, 2011 Biblica
Used by permission of Hodder & Stoughton Ltd, an Hachette uk company.
All rights reserved. 'niv' is a registered trademark of Biblica uk trademark number 1448790.

Scripture quotations marked nkjv are taken f rom the New King James Version®.
Copyright © 1982 by Thomas Nelson. Used by permission. All rights reserved.

Scripture quotations marked nlt are taken from the Holy Bible, New Living Translation,
copyright ©1996, 2004, 2015 by Tyndale House Foundation. Used by permission of Tyndale House
Publishers, Carol Stream, Illinois 60188. All rights reserved.

Cover design by Bekah Grace

Contents

Welcome to the Wellbeing Adventure..v

A is for Acceptance 2

B is for Breath.. 4

C is for Compassion... 6

D is for Dwell.. 8

E is for Empty..10

F is for Family..12

G is for Growth..14

H is for Hope...16

I is for Interests..18

J is for Joy... 20

K is for Kindness 22

L is for Lament.. 24

M is for Meditation.. 26

N is for Names 28

O is for One 30

P is for Present... 32

Q is for Quiet... 34

R is for Renew 36

S is for Simple.. 38

T is for Thanks. 40

U is for Unite 42

V is for Values. 44

W is for Wait 46

X Marks the Spot. 48

Y is for You 50

Z is for Zzz 52

Notes 54

Welcome to the Wellbeing Adventure

Here are some ideas to help you as you teach others about wellbeing from a Christian perspective. This Toolkit is a companion to the *A–Z of Wellbeing for Children*.

You will need to take a look at each chapter in the companion book to be able to use these resources effectively. This resource book gives clear ideas about using the *A–Z of Wellbeing* in a school setting such as an assembly (act of worship) or class lesson, or even a children's or young people's group at church. You could also incorporate some ideas into your church services, making it accessible for everyone.

A host of images and activities have been produced to accompany this resource book, which are available for you to download here:

https://www.authenticmedia.co.uk/az-of-wellbeing

Throughout the book we will reference the images available to download, with a corresponding number. To access the images simply go to the web page and navigate to the one you need. Then you can use them however you wish – for projecting on a screen, or printing as many as you need for use in your groups.

The *A–Z of Wellbeing for Children* was written with reference to the International Children's Bible Anglicised Edition. We would recommend using this version alongside the book as it is designed to be accessible and easy for children to understand.

The first part of each chapter takes an approach that can be used with a larger group, for example, an assembly or class, but could easily be adapted to a smaller group. The second section of each chapter has additional activities for smaller groups or individuals to follow an assembly or lesson. You can adapt the resources depending on your situation.

The Wellbeing journey taken here employs the language of the Five Ways to Wellbeing[1] which are widely used in mental health circles.

These five ways are:

Connecting
Learning
Getting Active
Taking Notice
Giving

For each letter of the alphabet, we are suggesting a word that embodies a wellbeing concept.

The Connect part of the chapter gives you two ways of introducing the wellbeing word to help your group engage with it.

The Learn section has a Jesus story with an accompanying image to help you present it.

The Get Active section gives you some suggestions of activities to help embed the concept.

The Take Notice section encourages the group to take a quiet moment and reflect on how they are feeling and on what the Bible says about the word they have been looking at.

In the final section, Give, we suggest a way of sharing what has been learned with others and there is a blessing to give away too.

After reading the chapter in the accompanying book please feel free to use any of the ideas in this resource book to help you as you share the wellbeing journey with others.

Enjoy the Wellbeing adventure!

Ruth and Debbie x

A is for Acceptance

 ## CONNECT

- Talk about the word 'acceptance'. Maybe share stories about the best present you have ever received and why it was important to accept it.
- Ask how it feels to be chosen (accepted) for a team.

 ## LEARN

- We believe the stories of Jesus are brilliant ways of illustrating wellbeing. Use the story of Peter being accepted in Luke 5:1–11. You can read out the version written in the *A–Z of Wellbeing for Children*. There is an image that you can project on the screen while you read (see '01 Acceptance illustration').

GET ACTIVE

- Encourage everyone to pull a few faces using their eyebrows and mouth position to show different emotions.
- Explain that God loves us and looks lovingly on us. He accepts us.

 ## TAKE NOTICE

- Use a picture of lots of different cups (see '02 Various cups'). Each one is different, just like us and although we have favourites, God doesn't. He loves and accepts everyone who comes to him.
- Invite everyone to close their eyes and settle comfortably. Ask everyone to imagine God holding their lives like a cup, chosen and precious to him. Enjoy knowing you are accepted and loved.

 # GIVE

- Ask the group to think about someone who might need to feel more accepted. How might they be able to help?

A BLESSING OF ACCEPTANCE

> *You are accepted*
> *I am too*
> *God loves your face*
> *He made you, you*
> *Thank you, God*
> *That I am me*
> *Your love is enough*
> *It sets me free*

 # ADDITIONAL IDEAS FOR SMALL GROUPS OR INDIVIDUALS

- Use mirrors to try out different expressions and chat about how we use our faces to show how we feel.
- Chat about different presents they have received and how the present-giver would have felt if they hadn't accepted the gift.
- Ask them how they feel when they aren't accepted. Should that change the way they treat other people?
- Print off the picture of Peter in the boat with the blessing prayer for a colouring activity (see '03 Peter and fish colouring').
- Print off the activity sheet for Acceptance with space to draw a self-portrait and doodle some ideas of ways they can help others to feel accepted (see '04 Activity sheet for A').

B is for Breath

 **CONNECT**

- Talk about how we breathe all the time and hardly ever notice.
- Ask about times when we do notice our breathing; for example, when we are running, feeling anxious, trying to calm ourselves.

 **LEARN**

- Use the story of Jesus' baptism from Matthew 3:1–17. Read out the version written in the *A–Z of Wellbeing for Children*, which highlights the link between our breathing and God's Holy Spirit life.
- There is an image that you can project on the screen while you read (see '05 Breathe illustration').

 GET ACTIVE

- Use balloons or bubbles to talk about the different things breath can do.
- Using straws and ping pong balls set up a race between two volunteers.

 TAKE NOTICE

- The Bible says that each breath is a gift from God. He breathed life into us and the Holy Spirit is like wind or breath.
- Invite everyone to close their eyes and settle comfortably. The Hebrew name for God sounds like breathing in and out. Yahweh. Ask everyone to quietly say the name as they breathe in and out.

 **GIVE**

- Practise doing some calming breathing activities together in a group and see if it is more helpful than trying to do it on your own. We can help each other even with breathing!

A BLESSING FOR YOUR BREATHS

> *Your love is*
> *in every breath I take*
> *When I'm asleep*
> *and when I'm awake*
> *Breathe in*
> *Breathe out*
> *and then repeat*
> *God fills me up*
> *from my head to my feet*

 ### ADDITIONAL IDEAS FOR SMALL GROUPS OR INDIVIDUALS

- Discuss times when they have been aware of their breathing, perhaps when they've been doing physical activity or when they were nervous.
- Using straws and blobs of paint, invite them to make abstract pieces of art by blowing the paint through the straws.
- If there is space, invite everyone to lie on the floor and place their hands on their chests, breathing in and out calmly and slowly and thinking about their breathing. Chat to them afterwards about whether they felt any different after doing that. Calmer? More peaceful?
- Print off the colouring picture of Jesus coming out of the water at his baptism (see '06 Jesus is baptised colouring').
- Print off the activity sheet with balloon patterns to colour (see '07 Activity sheet for B'). Invite them to silently spend some time with this, telling them beforehand how long they have so they can relax into it. Invite them to notice their breathing as they colour. Does it slow down? Maybe play some calming music to distract them from chatting.

C is for Compassion

CONNECT

- Tell a story about an act of compassion. It could be about someone being compassionate to you, or a story about children being compassionate towards each other in school or church.
- Highlight a charity that works in a country suffering from war or drought. Compassion can mean to suffer with someone, or share their difficult moment.

LEARN

- Use the story of Jesus healing Jairus's daughter from Mark 5:21–43. Read out the version written in the *A–Z of Wellbeing for Children*.
- There is an image that you can project on the screen while you read (see '08 Compassion illustration').

GET ACTIVE

- Explain that in order to be a compassionate person it is important to try to understand what other people are feeling. Show on the screen lots of emojis (see '09 Emojis to choose from') showing different emotions. Ask them what they think each one represents.
- Take a few moments to share with the person next to you a time when someone showed you compassion or you showed compassion to someone else.

TAKE NOTICE

- The Bible says God is full of compassion, 'slow to get angry' and full of love (Ps. 103:8, nlt).
- Invite everyone to close their eyes and settle comfortably. Picture God looking at you with love and being compassionate towards you like the best friend ever.

 **GIVE**

- Try listening carefully to a friend today. Or maybe make a card or gift for someone who needs a compassionate friend.

A BLESSING OF COMPASSION

*May you feel
more compassion
from the God who is love
He's beside
Walking with you
God, here below
Not just up above*

 ADDITIONAL IDEAS FOR SMALL GROUPS OR INDIVIDUALS

- Chat about a time when someone showed you compassion. How did it feel?
- Can you think of a time when you showed compassion to someone else?
- You could have a go at making homemade pizzas and name each topping after an emotion. Often we are a mixture of emotions, like toppings on a pizza, not just one.
- Print off the colouring sheet of Jesus showing compassion to Jairus's daughter (see '10 Jairus's daughter colouring').
- Print off the activity sheet and use it to help everyone think about their mixture of emotions (see '11 Activity sheet for C').

D is for Dwell

CONNECT

- Talk about the word 'dwell'. Discuss how we all have our favourite places to sit at home.
- Do they have another home they like to visit? What makes them feel welcome there?

LEARN

- Use the story of Mary and Martha from Luke 10:38–42. You can read out the version written in the *A–Z of Wellbeing for Children*.
- There is an image that you can project on the screen while you read (see '12 Dwell illustration').

GET ACTIVE

- See if everyone can stay completely still for a whole minute.
- Chat with the person next to you about how you could make this room a more comfortable and welcoming space.

TAKE NOTICE

- To be still in God's presence can be called 'dwelling' there. To help you do this you can use psalms like Psalm 103 (see prayer in the back of the *A–Z of Wellbeing for Children*). Some people like to make time to dwell with God every day. Suggest tips to make this easier; for example, having a notebook, a pen, a Bible and maybe a little battery-operated candle.
- Invite everyone to close their eyes and settle comfortably. Ask them to completely relax, thinking about how they put all their weight on whatever they are sitting on and how we need to lean on God.

 **GIVE**

- Think about ways you can make people feel really welcome and at home when they visit you.

A BLESSING FOR DWELLBEING

> *Dwell in me, God*
> *as I choose to dwell in you*
> *Help me remember*
> *you dwell in me too*
>
> *So make yourself at home*
> *in my heart and in my head*
> *in every moment of this day*
> *until I get back into bed*

 ADDITIONAL IDEAS FOR SMALL GROUPS OR INDIVIDUALS

- Have a go at making a sand timer using plastic bottles, sand and sticky tape. By changing the size of the hole and amount of sand, see if you can make one that lasts exactly 1 minute. Then use this to time yourself sitting still and dwelling in God's presence.
- Play a game of musical statues with a difference. Stop the music for a whole minute, or maybe just 30 seconds! Can everyone stay still for that long?
- Chat about what makes a good host. Why do you feel at home in some places? How can you make people feel more welcome when they visit you?
- Print off the colouring sheet showing Mary enjoying time being still and listening to Jesus (see '13 Mary at Jesus's feet colouring').
- Print off the prayer activity sheet highlighting parts of Psalm 103 (see '14 Activity sheet for D').

E is for Empty

CONNECT

- Talk about the difference between full and empty and how sometimes empty can be good. Empty hands are free to do something for someone else.
- If we are full of our own achievements, it can be difficult for others to be friends with us.

LEARN

- Use the story of the rich young man from Matthew 19:16–23. You can read out the version written in the *A–Z of Wellbeing for Children*.
- There is an image that you can project on the screen while you read (see '15 Empty illustration').

GET ACTIVE

- Hold your hands out like a cup. They are empty. Christians believe God asks us to come with empty hands so that he can provide what we need. You can't come to God with a big list of things that will make God love you more. He loves you anyway.
- Have two volunteers. Give one lots of boxes to hold. Then bring out a box of chocolates. Use it to illustrate how when we are empty, we are ready to receive from God, but if we think we have it all, we have no room for his treasures in our lives.

TAKE NOTICE

- Ephesians 1:23: 'Christ fills everything in every way.'
- Invite everyone to close their eyes and settle comfortably. Ask the group to hold their hands out and imagine all their worries are being held there. Then ask them to turn them over and imagine handing over their worries. Talking about our worries with a trusted adult or with God can be really helpful.

 **GIVE**

- Can you give someone the gift of your time and attention today at some point, even if you feel a bit too busy for them?

A BLESSING OF EMPTINESS

> *May you be empty enough*
> *to receive the gift God brings today*
> *And may you get filled with his love*
> *as you slow down, show up and pray*

 **ADDITIONAL IDEAS FOR SMALL GROUPS OR INDIVIDUALS**

- Chat about the word 'empty', how it can be negative and positive. Focus on the positive.
- Make an origami paper box with beautiful paper to give as a gift. Leave it empty so that it is useful!
- Take some time to tidy out a cupboard or drawer, giving away what you don't need to someone who will find it useful.
- Print off the colouring sheet showing the rich young man with his hands and his mind so full of things that he found it hard to give them up and follow Jesus (see '16 Rich young man colouring').
- Print off the spot the difference activity sheet (see '17 Activity sheet for E').

F is for Family

CONNECT

- To introduce the word 'family', talk about the people we feel comfortable with. That might be our families, or friendship groups, or a club we attend, or a church.
- It's good to be in a group that accept you as you are, like a family, but love you enough to want to help you be the best version of you.

LEARN

- Use the story of the four friends who lowered the paralysed man through the roof to Jesus from Mark 2:1–12. You can read out the version written in the *A–Z of Wellbeing for Children*.
- There is an image that you can project on the screen while you read (see '18 Family illustration').

GET ACTIVE

- Get a group of volunteers (or everyone, if that's possible!) and give each one a strip of paper and 20 seconds to write their name on the paper and draw a doodle of themselves. Then staple them together in a paper chain, illustrating how they are linked and represent family in your school setting.
- There are lots of games that illustrate working together. Volunteers could hold hands in a line, passing a hoop along, climbing through it as it reaches them. Show how much easier it is when someone else helps who isn't in the line.

TAKE NOTICE

- In the Bible it says, 'God sets the lonely in families' (Ps. 68:6, niv).
- Invite everyone to close their eyes and settle comfortably. Encourage them to think of five people important to them and use the fingers on one hand to help them to remember to pray for them.

 **GIVE**

- Is there someone you could include more who often gets left out?

A BLESSING FOR FAMILY

> Father, who holds us
> Son, who enfolds us
> Spirit, who gives love a voice
> Teach us to love
> Like you first loved us
> To be deep-hearted family
> Not as duty but choice[2]

 ADDITIONAL IDEAS FOR SMALL GROUPS OR INDIVIDUALS

- Chat about the word 'family'. Who is like family to you, and why?
- Make a paper chain of people by folding paper like a fan and cutting out one person.
- Chat about which clubs you are involved with or would like to get involved with.
- Print off the colouring sheet showing the four friends lowering the paralysed man through the roof (see '19 Friends of paralysed man colouring').
- Print off the gallery activity sheet where they can draw people who are important to them (see '20 Activity sheet for F').

G is for Growth

 CONNECT

- Bring in a plant. Depending on your gardening skills, this could be a demonstration of good or terrible ability to achieve growth!
- Ask the group what their favourite plants or trees are.

 LEARN

- Use the parable about the sower, or actually the four soils, that Jesus told from Matthew 13:1–23. You can read out the version written in the *A–Z of Wellbeing for Children*.
- There is an image that you can project on the screen while you read (see '21 Growth illustration').

GET ACTIVE

- Talk about what a plant needs to thrive. Have some seeds, along with compost and pots, for volunteers to come up and plant.
- Show a picture or pictures of different seeds and the plants they grow up into (see '22 Seeds and trees').

TAKE NOTICE

- A seed has to fall into the ground and die before it can grow into something amazing. Jesus explained his own death and resurrection in John 12:23–24 in terms of a kernel of wheat dying then producing many seeds.
- Invite everyone to close their eyes and settle comfortably. God sees your life like a seed full of potential. Picture all the good things you can do, growing inside you, and thank God for them.

 **GIVE**

- Giving flowers is a lovely way to say you are thinking about someone. If that's not possible, a drawing of flowers lasts even longer. Ask the group who they could encourage this week.

A BLESSING FOR GROWTH

> *Great gardener of my soul and mind*
> *Please come and clear the weeds you find*
> *You are the soil*
> *I am the seed*
> *and your deep love*
> *is all I need*

 ADDITIONAL IDEAS FOR SMALL GROUPS OR INDIVIDUALS

- Give everyone a little seed to hold. Can they guess what it will become? Christians believe God puts within us our gifts, talents and potential.
- Plant something easy to grow, for example, beans or cress, and enjoy talking about the miracle of transformation as they grow.
- Talk to the group about whether your school has a gardening club they could join, or maybe even start.
- Print off and colour in this picture of the four different soils in the parable of the sower (see '23 Four soils colouring').
- Print off the activity sheet to design their own garden (see '24 Activity sheet for G').

H is for Hope

CONNECT

- Talk about the word 'hope' and how we use it today.
- The Bible uses the word 'hope' in a different way. Psalm 42:5–6 says, 'Why am I so sad? Why am I so upset? I should put my hope in God. I should keep praising him, My Saviour and my God.' Hope is a positive and definite thing, rather than a maybe.

LEARN

- Use the parable of the lost coin that Jesus told from Luke 15:8–10. You can read out the version written in the *A–Z of Wellbeing for Children*.
- There is an image that you can project on the screen while you read (see '25 Hope illustration').

GET ACTIVE

- Share how some people paint stones with the word 'HOPE' and varnish them, then leave them for people to find. This is something they might like to try.
- To illustrate how the Bible says that 'hope does not disappoint us' (Rom. 5:5, gnt), ask for three volunteers and give them each a box to open. Ask them what they hope is inside. Put something nice (a wrapped bar of chocolate, for example) in every box.

TAKE NOTICE

- The Bible talks about hope being an 'anchor for the soul' (Heb. 6:19). Talk about how when storms come, the anchor keeps the ship from crashing into the harbour wall or going off course.
- Invite everyone to close their eyes and settle comfortably. Pray for places around the world and close to home that need hope.

 ## GIVE

- Watch out for any of your friends looking like they need a little bit more hope today, and offer them a smile or some help.

A BLESSING FOR HOPE

> *May the God of all peace*
> *fill you with hope*
> *that is more than wishes that*
> *may come true*
> *But truth and love*
> *and a knowing deep down*
> *that God will always, always*
> *love you*

 ## ADDITIONAL IDEAS FOR SMALL GROUPS OR INDIVIDUALS

- Have a go at painting the word 'HOPE' on stones and varnishing them. Put them outside where people might find them just when they need them.
- You could also paint stones with other encouraging words or Bible verses on them, and put them in a prayer jar to prompt different types of prayers.
- Make a collage of things that bring the group hope. Cut out pictures from magazines and encourage them to include positive and hopeful words in the artwork.
- Print off the picture of the coin lost in the woman's house to colour (see '26 Lost coin colouring').
- Print off the 'can you spot' activity sheet (see '27 Activity sheet for H').

I is for Interests

CONNECT

- Bring in a prop to demonstrate a hobby or interest you have, explaining why you make time for it.
- See how quickly the group can name twenty hobbies.

LEARN

- Use the parable of the talents that Jesus told from Matthew 25:14–30. You can read out the version written in the *A–Z of Wellbeing for Children*.
- There is an image that you can project on the screen while you read (see '28 Interests illustration').

GET ACTIVE

- Name some clubs in school or hobbies children might have, getting them to stand up if they've ever taken part in them.
- Prepare beforehand to hold up some pieces of work from school (art, numeracy, creative writing, etc.), pointing out that each of us has talents and interests and it's important to figure out what is it that you enjoy and are good at.

TAKE NOTICE

- Sometimes hobbies are calming because they are repetitive, like knitting or crochet. Another repetitive, calming activity is to choose part of a Bible verse and repeat it in your head. It will help you remember it and also help you to focus on something good and uplifting. Philippians 4:8 says, 'continue to think about the things that are good and worthy of praise. Think about the things that are true and honorable and right and pure and beautiful and respected.'
- Invite everyone to close their eyes and settle comfortably. Think about all the things that you like doing, and picture God smiling at you as you do them.

GIVE

- If you have a hobby you like, why not ask around to see if anyone would like to form a club so that you can share that hobby with others?

A BLESSING FOR YOUR INTERESTS

> *God, who made all people*
> *and everything we see*
> *Please recreate wellbeing*
> *right here, right now, in me*

ADDITIONAL IDEAS FOR SMALL GROUPS OR INDIVIDUALS

- Discuss hobbies that the group already have and what they would like to have a go at. Discuss which subjects they really enjoy at school too.
- Make a poster of the clubs at your school to advertise them more widely.
- Discuss why we think making things brings us joy. Get the group to talk about something they did that they are proud of. Could it be because God is a Creator God and he made us to enjoy creativity?
- Print off the colouring picture of the bags of gold from the parable (see '29 Bags of gold colouring').
- Print off the wordsearch activity sheet (see '30 Activity sheet for I').

J is for Joy

CONNECT

- Talk about what makes you happy. Explain that being happy all the time isn't possible, but it is possible to find contentment or joy even when the circumstances don't make you happy. Talk about how joy can exist alongside other feelings like sadness.
- Play a piece of music that has a melody that sounds sad but a deeper bass note that feels steady. Talk about the bass note of joy even if the tune playing feels sad. Quite a lot of classical music can be used for this, including Barber's *Adagio for Strings* or Elgar's 'Nimrod' from the *Enigma Variations*.

LEARN

- For a story that contains joy and a problem, read the story of the wedding at Cana from John 2:1–11. You can read it from the servant's perspective found in the *A–Z of Wellbeing for Children*.
- There is an image that you can project on the screen while you read (see '31 Joy illustration').

GET ACTIVE

- Have a go at something fun like a Mexican wave.
- List some 'fun' activities. The group can agree (thumbs up), disagree (thumbs down) or put their hands out flat if they aren't sure. Make the point that different activities bring joy to different people.

TAKE NOTICE

- In Galatians 5:22–23, joy is one of the nine fruits that comes from having God's Spirit in charge. List them, maybe with actions for each one.
- Invite everyone to close their eyes and settle comfortably. Think of something that made you smile this week.

 **GIVE**

- Ask the group what they could do to bring someone else joy. Share ideas.

A BLESSING FOR JOY

> There is joy
> in every detail
> of this world that you have made
> Lord, help me hear your joy notes
> in every place I've worked and played

 ADDITIONAL IDEAS FOR SMALL GROUPS OR INDIVIDUALS

- Discuss the difference between joy and happiness.
- If appropriate, go outside and have a run, a skip or even just lie down and watch the clouds.
- Discuss ways of bringing joy to others, and plan together how and when they will do that.
- Print off the colouring sheet of the servant at the wedding at Cana (see '32 Wedding at Cana colouring').
- Print off the activity sheet with ideas about bringing joy to others (see '33 Activity sheet for J').

K is for Kindness

 ## CONNECT

- Talk about an act of kindness you've experienced recently.
- Try to find a story in the news about someone being kind to share with the group.

 ## LEARN

- Use the parable Jesus told of the Good Samaritan from Luke 10:25–37. You can read it from the traveller's perspective found in the *A–Z of Wellbeing for Children*.
- There is an image that you can project on the screen while you read (see '34 Kindness illustration').

 ## GET ACTIVE

- Suggest you all have an acts of kindness (AoK) day. Ask the children for ideas of kind things they could do.
- Ask for volunteers to make posters to advertise the day. Suggest this could be a regular event.

 ## TAKE NOTICE

- The Bible says in Matthew 22:39 that we are to love others as we love ourselves. Think about whether we are kind to ourselves.
- Invite everyone to close their eyes and settle comfortably. Think of a really kind thing someone said or did to you this week and thank them later if you can.

GIVE

- What one kind thing could you do today?

A BLESSING OF KINDNESS

> *God, you are so kind*
> *Please fill my heart and mind*
> *so I can show real kindness too*
> *and my kind acts will point to YOU*

 ADDITIONAL IDEAS FOR SMALL GROUPS OR INDIVIDUALS

- Chat about acts of kindness that the group have experienced.
- Chat about how it changes your day when someone is kind to you.
- Make a list of the ways God is kind from Psalm 139 and Psalm 23.
- Print off the picture of the Good Samaritan to colour (see '35 Good Samaritan colouring').
- Print off the poster activity sheet for an Acts of Kindness day (see '36 Activity sheet for K').

L is for Lament

CONNECT

- Ask the group what they do when they are feeling sad. What helps? Maybe explain what you do.
- Explain the word 'Lament'. It is a way of expressing yourself when you feel sad. Sometimes people think they have to hide their sad feelings, but that doesn't usually help.

LEARN

- Use the story of the death and resurrection of Lazarus from John 11:1–46. You can read the version found in the *A–Z of Wellbeing for Children*.
- There is an image that you can project on the screen while you read (see '37 Lament illustration').

GET ACTIVE

- Have something very heavy at the front and pretend you can't lift it. Ask for volunteers to help you. Explain that if you'd just kept trying on your own, you might have hurt yourself. Use this as an illustration to encourage the group to ask for help if they are feeling sad.
- Listen to a piece of music that feels emotional. Encourage the group to close their eyes and hand over to God the things that make them sad.

TAKE NOTICE

- Psalm 34:18 says, 'The Lord is close to the brokenhearted.'
- Invite everyone to close their eyes and settle comfortably. Think of a time you felt sad or something that makes you feel sad today. Talk to God about it.

 **GIVE**

- Look out for a friend who seems sad today and spend some time listening to them or just give them a smile.

A BLESSING FOR YOUR LAMENT

> *Whatever you are feeling*
> *Super-happy*
> *or so sad*
> *Know that Jesus knows you best,*
> *Knows every feeling that you've had*
> *So tell him what is on your mind*
> *Worry, sadness, fear*
> *Whatever you are feeling*
> *May you know that he is near*

 **ADDITIONAL IDEAS FOR SMALL GROUPS OR INDIVIDUALS**

- Share stories about times when you have found strength from others or from God when you've been sad.
- Enjoy listening to some emotional classical / worship music. Invite them to sit or lie comfortably, or doodle while they listen.
- If you know of churches or support groups for people struggling with sadness locally, discuss ways you could help them that might bring a smile in their difficult times.
- Print off the picture of Mary and Martha to colour (see '38 Mary and Martha colouring').
- Print off the activity sheet of helpful Bible verses, decorate them and make it into a little booklet (see '39 Activity sheet for L').

M is for Meditation

 **CONNECT**

- Ask who is good at worrying. Explain how worry is just like meditating, going over and over one thing in our heads. Worrying is just focusing on one negative thing.
- Challenge the group to try meditating on something good instead. It is focusing on one positive thing.

 **LEARN**

- Use the story of Jesus teaching the disciples the Lord's Prayer from Luke 11:1–4. You can read the version found in the *A–Z of Wellbeing for Children*.
- There is an image that you can project on the screen while you read (see '40 Meditation illustration').

 GET ACTIVE

- Ask for a volunteer who is good at skipping. Meditating doesn't need to be done only when you are sitting still. Get the group to say a short Bible phrase in time to the skipping; for example, 'The Lord is my shepherd. I have everything I need' (Ps. 23:1); 'Love is patient and kind' (1 Cor. 13:4); 'Faith, hope and love . . . the greatest of these is love' (1 Cor. 13:13); 'You, Lord, give true peace' (Isa. 26:3).
- You could do this with a ball bouncing between volunteers. Or in time to someone hopping!

TAKE NOTICE

- Give a few examples of Bible verses or phrases that would be suitable for meditating on. Practise breathing in half the phrase and breathing out for the other half, saying it in your heads.
- Invite everyone to close their eyes and settle comfortably. Take a phrase like 'you are loved and accepted' and breathe it in and out for a minute together.

 **GIVE**

- 'Love your neighbor as you love yourself' (Matt. 22:39) is a great verse to meditate on and encourage the group to take care of each other.

A BLESSING FOR MEDITATION

> *May your quiet moments*
> *be filled with his Word*
> *May your head be clear of worries*
> *so the truth can be heard*

 ADDITIONAL IDEAS FOR SMALL GROUPS OR INDIVIDUALS

- Help each person to pick a Bible phrase from a prepared list, and to spend 2 minutes silently breathing it in and out. Suggest they think of it regularly during the day.
- Find fun ways to meditate on the Bible. For example, repeating it while skipping, hopping, bouncing a ball against a wall or making up actions to it.
- Give each person a notebook to begin journaling. Discuss great ways to journal – writing out the Bible verse, using doodles, colours and stickers to decorate it and make it more memorable.
- Print off the picture of the disciple asking about prayer (see '41 Disciple asks how to pray colouring').
- Print off the Lord's Prayer activity sheet (see '42 Activity sheet for M').

N is for Names

 ## CONNECT

- Ask who likes their name.
- See if anyone knows what their name means.

 ## LEARN

- Use the story of Zacchaeus from Luke 19:1–10 to illustrate the impact of Jesus calling us by name. You can read the version found in the *A–Z of Wellbeing for Children*.
- There is an image that you can project on the screen while you read (see '43 Names illustration').

 ## GET ACTIVE

- Find out who in the room has the longest and shortest names.
- See how many names or descriptions for God you can come up with, maybe one for each letter of the alphabet.

 ## TAKE NOTICE

- Isaiah 43:1 says, 'Don't be afraid, because I have saved you. I have called you by name, and you are mine.' God knows our names.
- Invite everyone to close their eyes and settle comfortably. Say your own name quietly several times. Say thank you that God knows your name.

 ## GIVE

- Do you know all the names of the people in your class / club / church? If not, try to find out the names of the people you don't know.

A BLESSING FOR YOUR NAME

> *Jesus, name above all names*
> *Thanks that you know my name too*
> *and that every person that I see*
> *is known and loved by you*

 ADDITIONAL IDEAS FOR SMALL GROUPS OR INDIVIDUALS

- Give the group resources to make name plates to go on their bedroom doors or on their desks.
- Find out if any of the group know why they have the name they were given.
- Play a praying game where you pray for someone beginning with each letter of the alphabet.
- Print off the picture of Zacchaeus up a tree to colour (see '44 Zaccheus in tree colouring').
- Print off the A–Z activity sheet (see '45 Activity sheet for N').

O is for One

 **CONNECT**

- Ask the group what they would prefer: lots of friends who don't know you very well, or one friend who really cares.
- Talk about how sometimes we focus too much on having lots of things; for example, toys, food, friends. People are sometimes much happier with just one thing that they treasure than lots of things they aren't bothered about.

 **LEARN**

- Use the story of Jesus spending time with the Samaritan woman at the well from John 4:4–42. You can read the version found in the *A–Z of Wellbeing for Children*.
- There is an image that you can project on the screen while you read (see '46 One illustration').

GET ACTIVE

- Give them 1 minute to chat to the person next to them and find out one thing they didn't already know about them.
- Ask them to think of one person who has made their lives better. Perhaps share a few examples from the group.

TAKE NOTICE

- Can they think of the names of one individual that Jesus helped? For example, Zacchaeus, Samaritan woman, Nicodemus, Mary Magdalene, Peter, James, John, Jairus's daughter, paralysed man, blind Bartimaeus, etc.
- Invite everyone to close their eyes and settle comfortably. Ask everyone to think of one saying or verse that has helped them.

 **GIVE**

- What one thing could they do today to make someone else's day better?

A BLESSING FOR THE ONE

> *Help me to love you, Lord*
> *with all my heart and soul*
> *Make all the broken bits of me*
> *into one loved and loving whole*

 **ADDITIONAL IDEAS FOR SMALL GROUPS OR INDIVIDUALS**

- Chat about what one thing is really important to each person in the group.
- Discuss ways of simplifying life. Perhaps tidying their bedrooms and giving to charity those things we don't need anymore. Maybe choosing one thing to give away as a gift to someone else.
- Talk about people who have had an influence on our lives, who have helped us to become better people and invested time in us.
- Print off the picture of the woman at the well to colour (see '47 Woman at the well colouring').
- Print off the prayer activity sheet (see '48 Activity sheet for O').

P is for Present

 **CONNECT**

- Being in the present is good for us. Ask everyone what they noticed when they were travelling to school. Talk about how it's good to be present, to think about what's around you, rather than worry about the future or the past.
- Ask for two volunteers who don't have food allergies. Give them each a grape and ask one to eat it quickly and the other one really slowly. At the end, ask them to describe the grape. Hopefully the one who took it slowly will have noticed more about its sweetness, texture, juiciness, etc.

 **LEARN**

- Use the story of Peter walking on the water with Jesus from Matthew 14:22–36. You can read the version found in the *A–Z of Wellbeing for Children*.
- There is an image that you can project on the screen while you read (see '49 Present illustration').

 **GET ACTIVE**

- Give everyone 30 seconds to have a really good look around. Then ask them questions about things on the walls behind them, noises that they may have heard, what the teacher at the back was wearing.
- Play some restful music and invite everyone to calmly enjoy the moment.

 **TAKE NOTICE**

- God doesn't want us to focus on the worries of tomorrow. He wants us to enjoy each moment he gives us. Psalm 118:24 says, 'This is the day the Lord has made. Let us rejoice and be glad today!'

- Invite everyone to close their eyes and settle comfortably. Think about massive things and tiny details in God's creation. Invite everyone to look out of the window if they can and notice the sky, then to look at their fingerprints and focus on the details of the swirling patterns.

GIVE

- When someone tells you something today, try to be really present. Don't think about what you are going to say next. Focus on what they are saying and how they may be feeling.

A BLESSING TO BE PRESENT

> *God of the past and the future*
> *I choose to be present today*
> *Help me to be fully here and receive*
> *the gift of your presence, I pray*

ADDITIONAL IDEAS FOR SMALL GROUPS OR INDIVIDUALS

- In pairs, invite them to talk about something for a whole minute while the other one listens, just listens, and doesn't interrupt. Chat afterwards about how it was different.
- Sit quietly, then chat about what they could hear and smell and what they were most focused on.
- Discuss when it might be even more important to be 'present' – when you are riding your bike, crossing the road, writing a story, drawing a picture. What happens when we are thinking about the past or the future?
- Print off the picture of Peter walking on water to colour (see '50 Peter walking on water colouring').
- Print off the activity sheet to help them observe things at a distance, 'zoom out', and the details of things close up, 'zoom in' (see '51 Activity sheet for P').

Q is for Quiet

 **CONNECT**

- Ask the group to put their hands up if they have trouble being quiet. Talk about how some people are naturally quiet. They are often better listeners.
- Have a go at being quiet, just for 30 seconds. Ask who enjoyed the quiet.

 **LEARN**

- Use the story of Jesus stilling the storm from Mark 4:35–41. You can read the version found in the *A–Z of Wellbeing for Children*.
- There is an image that you can project on the screen while you read (see '52 Quiet illustration').

GET ACTIVE

- Pop up a tent and fill it with cushions. Invite a volunteer to come and try it out. Ask them how it feels. Tell them they have to be quiet in that space. Suggest they make cosy, quiet dens at home; places where they are allowed to read and colour but not use technology.
- Ask the group when it is important to be quiet; for example, when you are working or concentrating, when someone is poorly or sleeping, when you are watching a wild bird or animal and don't want to frighten it away.

 TAKE NOTICE

- In Zephaniah 3:17 it says, 'The Lord your God is with you. The mighty One will save you. The Lord will be happy with you. You will rest in his love.' In some types of Bible it says 'He will quiet you with His love' (nkjv).
- Invite everyone to close their eyes and settle comfortably. Ask them to listen quietly to all the noises around them.

 **GIVE**

- Ask them who they know that enjoys a bit of quiet. Suggest that they offer to sit quietly with them next time they are together.

A BLESSING OF QUIET

> *Help me be calm enough to hear*
> *that you don't need all my busyness*
> *and words*
> *Quiet me with your love*
> *God who is near*

 **ADDITIONAL IDEAS FOR SMALL GROUPS OR INDIVIDUALS**

- While doing an activity, set a timer for every 5 minutes. When the timer pings, have 20 seconds of quiet. Chat afterwards about whether it was disruptive or good. Would it be useful to do this in other ways?
- Stay quiet for 3 minutes and write down everything you hear. Compare notes at the end.
- Chat as a group about what they might do at home that is a quiet activity. Perhaps reading or drawing. Talk about why it is important to have time away from our screens.
- Print off the picture of the disciple in the boat after the storm has been stilled to colour (see '53 Disciple after calming of storm colouring').
- Print off the colouring sheet of the letter Q as a quiet activity (see '54 Activity sheet for Q').

R is for Renew

CONNECT

- Introduce the concept of renewing by bringing in an example of something that has been upcycled and given a new purpose. Talk about why that is good for the planet.
- Ask who has ever fallen out with their friends. It's important to say sorry and have a fresh start. Often the new relationship is better than the old one once we say sorry and appreciate each other more.

LEARN

- Use the story of Nicodemus coming to Jesus and learning about needing to be renewed / born again from John 3:1–21. You can read the version found in the *A–Z of Wellbeing for Children*.
- There is an image that you can project on the screen while you read (see '55 Renew illustration').

GET ACTIVE

- Give three volunteers piles of identical pieces of 'rubbish' (for example, boxes, toilet rolls, plastic bottle lids, tin foil, scraps of wrapping paper, elastic bands, and so on), a pair of scissors and some tape and 5 minutes to transform them into a robot or some other object. Vote on the results.
- See if together you can come up with six ways to reuse a toilet roll tube; for example, use a squashed end for printing flower petals, make a pen holder, make a little robot, use them to plant out seedlings in the garden, etc.

TAKE NOTICE

- 2 Corinthians 5:17 says, 'If anyone belongs to Christ, then he is made new. The old things have gone; everything is made new!'

- Invite everyone to close their eyes and settle comfortably. Picture your life like a beautiful piece of art being made by God.

 ## GIVE

- Have a go at upcycling something as a meaningful present.

A BLESSING FOR RENEWING

> God, take all the scattered pieces
> of this broken place we live
> And carefully mosaic us
> into a new creation
> Designed to love and give

 ## ADDITIONAL IDEAS FOR SMALL GROUPS OR INDIVIDUALS

- As a group, make a huge poster with 'rubbish' – the pieces could be put together to spell out something like 'God makes everything new'.
- Everyone could bring an example from home of something recycled. Discuss why this is a good thing to do.
- Chat about times when we see renewal and how it makes us feel. Renewed friendships. A newly decorated bedroom. Something fixed that we can use again. The new life seen in springtime.
- Print off the picture of Nicodemus trying to understand being 'born again' to colour (see '56 Nicodemus at night colouring').
- Print off the word puzzle activity sheet (see '57 Activity sheet for R').

S is for Simple

CONNECT

- Talk about simplicity and how when things are simplified it can really help. For example, Ben Cohen and Jerry Greenfield paid $5 to learn how to make ice cream and today they own 'Ben and Jerry's' ice cream.
- Ask if we sometimes overcomplicate things. Sometimes a simple 'How can I help?' or even a smile can transform someone's day.

LEARN

- Use the story of the boy giving up his packed lunch to feed 5,000 people from John 6:1–15. You can read the version found in the *A–Z of Wellbeing for Children*.
- There is an image that you can project on the screen while you read (See '58 Simple illustration').

GET ACTIVE

- Play a simple game like blindfolding a volunteer and getting them to guess what an object could be simply by touch.
- Talk about how wearing glasses makes such a difference. Ask some volunteers who wear them to explain that difference to others. Glasses have been used in Britain since at least the fifteenth century, but people weren't easily able to afford them until after the Second World War. (From 1948 until 1986, the NHS offered free eye tests and glasses.)

TAKE NOTICE

- Read 1 John 4:9 to explain simply what Christianity is: 'This is how God showed his love to us: He sent his only Son into the world to give us life through him.'
- Invite everyone to close their eyes and settle comfortably. Ask everyone to think of one simple thing they have learned this week and to say a quiet thank you for it.

 **GIVE**

- What simple thing can you do today to make someone else's day better?

A BLESSING OF SIMPLICITY

> *May the God who simply loves you*
> *help you to live a simple way*
> *May you know exactly who you are*
> *and choose life with him today*

 ADDITIONAL IDEAS FOR SMALL GROUPS OR INDIVIDUALS

- Chat about what simple things they have learned that have made a big difference; for example, how to put their socks on, ways of telling the time, good tips on getting to sleep.
- Teach the group a simple craft that is really effective. Paper quilling to make flowers is impressive but simple.
- Look around the room and discuss ways it could be simplified to make learning easier; for example, book shelves tidied, drawers labelled, a place for lost property.
- Print off the picture of the loaves and fish to colour (see '59 Loaves and fish colouring').
- Print off the activity sheet about things they simply enjoy (see '60 Activity sheet for S').

T is for Thanks

 **CONNECT**

- Have a thank-you card to show everyone. Explain how being thanked makes such a difference.
- Having a grateful attitude can change the way we view things.

 LEARN

- Use the story of the ten lepers who were healed, but only one who came back to thank Jesus from Luke 17:11–19. You can read the version found in the *A–Z of Wellbeing for Children*.
- There is an image that you can project on the screen while you read (See '61 Thanks illustration').

GET ACTIVE

- Give everyone 1 minute to think of five things they are thankful for. Choose someone to give their examples. Then ask everyone to share their five with the person next to them.
- Put five things in a 'feely bag', one at a time, and get volunteers to guess what you are thankful for that relates to each of the five objects. For example, a glass, because you are thankful for clean water.

 TAKE NOTICE

- Read Philippians 4:6 and talk about how when we pray it's important to be thankful. 'Do not worry about anything. But pray and ask God for everything you need. And when you pray, always give thanks.'
- Invite everyone to close their eyes and settle comfortably. Ask everyone to think of as many things as they can that make them feel thankful today.

 **GIVE**

- Who could you say thank you to today?

A BLESSING OF THANKS

> *Thank you, Lord*
> *Just thank you loads*
> *For friends, for breath*
> *For frogs and toads*
> *For a tiny flower and a massive tree*
> *And thank you, Lord*
> *For making me, me*

 ADDITIONAL IDEAS FOR SMALL GROUPS OR INDIVIDUALS

- Chat about people, inventions, things in nature that you are all thankful for.
- Talk about the difference between people who see what there is to be thankful for in everything, and people who always just want more.
- Make thank-you cards that can be kept and used whenever needed.
- Print off the picture of the leper thanking Jesus to colour (see '62 Healed leper colouring').
- Print off the A–Z activity sheet (see '63 Activity sheet for T').

U is for Unite

CONNECT

- Talk about titles with the word 'united' in them; for example, Manchester United, United Kingdom, United States of America, United Nations. Ask the group why this word is used.
- Ask how teams make sure they have one purpose and are working together; for example, team meetings, rules, caring about what each other think or feel.

LEARN

- Use the story of the disciples arguing about who was the greatest from Mark 9:33–37. You can read the version found in the *A–Z of Wellbeing for Children*.
- There is an image that you can project on the screen while you read (see '64 Unite illustration').

GET ACTIVE

- Bring in an example of something made by mixing ingredients like a cake or a cappuccino, and ask what needs to come together to make it.
- Have a race, with two teams of volunteers. Having already scattered Lego bricks (or equivalent) around the room, get them to decide who will build and who will collect bricks. Give them a time limit to build the highest tower together.

TAKE NOTICE

- Psalm 133:1 says, 'It is good and pleasant when God's people live together in peace [unity].' The Bible talks about being 'peacemakers' too (Matt. 5:9, nkjv).
- Invite everyone to close their eyes and settle comfortably. Ask the group to picture one way they could help to bring peace when they see people quarrelling.

 **GIVE**

- Think about someone you might need to make friends with or say sorry to.

A BLESSING FOR UNITY

> *Just as you are three in one*
> *Unite us all in love*
> *Like the Father*
> *Spirit*
> *Son*

 ADDITIONAL IDEAS FOR SMALL GROUPS OR INDIVIDUALS

- Chat about what teams you are in, and the ways that those teams support each other and are united.
- Discuss the difference between groups of people who argue a lot and groups who live in unity.
- Discuss which flavours go well together; for example, orange and chocolate.
- Print off the picture of the disciples to colour (see '65 Disciples, Jesus and child colouring').
- Print off the code breaker activity sheet (see '66 Activity sheet for U').

V is for Values

CONNECT

- What are our values? Looking at the school's motto or the church's purpose statement can help to figure that out. Share yours.
- There are five values that are attached to wellbeing nationally. These are 'Connect', 'Learn', 'Get Active', 'Take Notice' and 'Give'. Talk about why these were chosen.

LEARN

- Use the parable Jesus told about the wise and foolish builders from Luke 6:46–49. You can read the version found in the *A–Z of Wellbeing for Children*.
- There is an image that you can project on the screen while you read (see '67 Values illustration').

GET ACTIVE

- Print out some sheets with words that represent possible values; for example, forgive, be kind, try hard, listen carefully. Ask for several older volunteers. Each one can put these values in order of how important they think they are. Talk about how we have different values.
- Ask whether their friends can see these values in the way these volunteers behave.

TAKE NOTICE

- When Jesus is asked about the most important commandment, he sums it all up in two sentences. Matthew 22:37–39 tells us: 'Jesus answered, "Love the Lord your God with all your heart, soul and mind." This is the first and most important command. And the second command is like the first: "Love your neighbour as you love yourself."'

- Invite everyone to close their eyes and settle comfortably. Ask each person to think about a value they have; for example, something that is really important to them and the way they behave.

GIVE

- Think about your values, and check that the way you treat other people today shows your values. If it doesn't, say sorry and start again.

A BLESSING FOR YOUR VALUES

> *May the God who values you so much*
> *show you what is great*
> *May you be someone who brings*
> *God's love,*
> *a really brilliant mate*

ADDITIONAL IDEAS FOR SMALL GROUPS OR INDIVIDUALS

- As a group, make little booklets to record different words that are important to them – their values.
- Discuss the parable of the wise and foolish builders. Jesus said it represented doing what he said (Luke 6:46). How do Christians build on the values of Jesus in their day-to-day lives?
- Discuss why the 'Five Ways to Wellbeing' are helpful to people: Connect, Learn, Get Active, Take Notice, Give.
- Print off the picture of the two houses from the parable to colour (see '68 Two houses colouring').
- Print off the activity sheet with ideas about how to make a poster displaying their own values (see '69 Activity sheet for V').

W is for Wait

CONNECT

- To help everyone think about the concept of waiting, start off the session by looking like you're going to speak, then waiting until it feels a bit uncomfortable. After a minute, ask how people felt.
- Ask what causes us to be impatient. What do we struggle to wait for?

LEARN

- Use the story of Jesus in the Garden of Gethsemane from Matthew 26:36–46. You can read the version found in the *A–Z of Wellbeing for Children*.
- There is an image that you can project on the screen while you read (see '70 Wait illustration').

GET ACTIVE

- Play a game with two volunteers. Each has a toilet roll unravelled with a wrapped treat on the paper at the end. They need to roll up the paper until it reaches them.
- Play a clapping game, where they copy your pattern. Eventually set a clapping pattern where there is a long pause included.

TAKE NOTICE

- Psalm 130:5–6 says: 'I wait for the Lord to help me. I trust his word. I wait for the Lord to help me more than night watchmen wait for the dawn.' (Explain what a night watchman is.)
- Invite everyone to close their eyes and settle comfortably. Ask the group to take notice of how they feel when they have to wait for something.

 **GIVE**

- Ask if there is anyone who has waited a long time for them to do what they said they would do; for example, tidy their room, play with them, teach them how to do something. Maybe this week they could keep that promise.

A BLESSING FOR WAITING

> *May you know that the God*
> *who waits for you*
> *waits with you*
> *And will give you patience*
> *as you wait for him too.*

 ADDITIONAL IDEAS FOR SMALL GROUPS OR INDIVIDUALS

- Discuss places and situations where waiting has to happen, and ways of making that more fun.
- Share about things you have waited a long time for but were worth it.
- Bake something, and while you wait for it in the oven, think of useful things to do, like tidy up, get the plates ready, make a drink.
- Print off the picture of the Garden of Gethsemane to colour (see '71 Garden of Gethsemane colouring').
- Print off the maze activity sheet (see '72 Activity sheet for W').

X Marks the Spot

 **CONNECT**

- Ask if everyone knows what it means to say 'X marks the spot'. Show a big treasure map.
- Talk about some of the significant moments and places in your life.

 **LEARN**

- To illustrate the importance of certain key moments in our lives, use the story of the soldier's reaction to Jesus when he is on the cross from Mark 15:37–39. You can read the version found in the *A–Z of Wellbeing for Children*.
- There is an image that you can project on the screen while you read (see '73 X marks the spot illustration').

 GET ACTIVE

- Explain that there is 'treasure' to be found in the room, and give a volunteer instructions about how many steps they need to take and different changes of direction to locate the treasure.
- Discuss with the person next to you one of your favourite moments in your life so far.

TAKE NOTICE

- Proverbs 2:2,4 tells us: 'Listen to wisdom. Try with all your heart to gain understanding . . . Search for it as you would for silver. Hunt for it like hidden treasure.'
- Invite everyone to close their eyes and settle comfortably. Think back over the last week or two (or even longer) and see if you can remember any special moments. These could be called treasure moments. It could be worth making a note of special moments and places. This is like making a treasure map of your life: 'X marks the spot'.

 **GIVE**

- If someone has made a big difference in your life and is included in one of your treasured moments, tell them, to encourage them.

A BLESSING FOR TREASURE

> Right here in the present my treasure lies
> God, you are my treasure
> You are my prize
> And wonder of wonders
> as I follow the clues
> I am finding that I am
> your treasure too

 ADDITIONAL IDEAS FOR SMALL GROUPS OR INDIVIDUALS

- Talk about your treasured moments and places where 'X marks the spot'.
- Make treasure maps, on paper or even 3D papier mâché ones!
- Make journals where you can record your treasured moments as they happen and remember them.
- Print off the picture of the soldier at the cross to colour (see '74 Soldier at the cross colouring').
- Print off the treasure map game to play (see '75 Activity sheet for X').

Y is for You

CONNECT

- This is all about you (not you, the teacher ... each person). Make three statements about yourself where one of them isn't true. Let everyone vote on which one they think is false.
- Ask for volunteers who have surprising facts about themselves and are willing to share them with everyone.

LEARN

- Use the story of Peter's chat with Jesus after the resurrection from John 21:1–17. You can read the version found in the *A–Z of Wellbeing for Children*.
- There is an image that you can project on the screen while you read (see '76 You illustration').

GET ACTIVE

- Have a voting game, choosing between two things; for example, food, TV programme, games, subjects at school. Highlight that we are different and that is fine.
- Arrange beforehand for some volunteers to bring in something they have made or won that they are proud of.

TAKE NOTICE

- Psalm 139:1–6 says:

    Lord, you have examined me. You know all about me. You know when I sit down and when I get up. You know my thoughts before I think them. You know where I go and where I lie down. You know well everything I do. Lord, even before I say a word, you already know what I am going to say. You are all around me – in front and in back. You have put your hand on me. Your knowledge is amazing to me. It is more than I can understand.

- Invite everyone to close their eyes and settle comfortably. Peter needed forgiving in order to move on and enjoy being who God made him to be. Are there things we need to be forgiven for?

 **GIVE**

- Think of something encouraging to say to everyone you meet today, and then actually say it!

A BLESSING FOR YOU

> *You*
> *are Unique*
> *There aren't*
> *two*
> *like you*
> *It's amazing that God loves me*
> *and sets me free*
> *and that*
> *you are the only you*
> *and I am the only me*

 ### ADDITIONAL IDEAS FOR SMALL GROUPS OR INDIVIDUALS

- Discuss the things that make each of you unique.
- Talk about why forgiveness is so important.
- Make a poster with parts of Psalm 139 on it.
- Print off the picture of Peter on the shore with Jesus to colour (see '77 Peter on the beach colouring').
- Print off the activity sheet that helps the group to think about what makes each of them special (see '78 Activity sheet for Y').

Z is for Zzz

CONNECT

- Ask everyone why sleep is important.
- Talk about what things we do in order to calm down at the end of the day and prepare for bed.

LEARN

- Use the story of the road to Emmaus from Luke 24:13–35. You can read the version found in the *A–Z of Wellbeing for Children*.
- There is an image that you can project on the screen while you read (see '79 Zzz illustration').

GET ACTIVE

- Counting sheep is supposed to help you get to sleep. How about learning a bit of the Bible instead, like Psalm 23? It's a lot, but you could do it bit by bit until you have memorised a whole psalm.
- The 'Prayer of Examen' has been used for centuries. It encourages you to look back on your day and think what there was to be thankful for, and where you noticed God's blessing and beauty. Then look back at what wasn't so good and say sorry, then let go of it. It helps you to learn something. Ask everyone to share with a partner one good and one bad thing from the past day or two.

TAKE NOTICE

- Psalm 63:6 says: 'I remember you while I'm lying in bed. I think about you through the night.'
- Invite everyone to close their eyes and settle comfortably. Ask what helps them get to sleep. Encourage them to relax and rest for a minute.

GIVE

- Pray for those who don't have a restful place to sleep tonight.

A BLESSING FOR SLEEP

> And so to sleep
> knowing God will keep
> you
> He will hold you
> because he knows you
> best of all
> However big
> However small
> He loves you
> Sees you
> Is ever near you
> This God of wellbeing
> will help you
> to be you
> So rest, just rest
> God knows what's best

ADDITIONAL IDEAS FOR SMALL GROUPS OR INDIVIDUALS

- Make a mobile with sheep decorations and Bible verses that are calming.
- Make and decorate a poster with Psalm 23 on it.
- Discuss helpful ways of getting to sleep.
- Print off the picture of the two disciples in Emmaus to colour (see '80 Two disciples in Emmaus colouring').
- Print off the A–Z activity sheet (see '81 Activity sheet for Z').

Notes

1. https.neweconomics.org.uk (accessed 8 May 2024).
2. Ruth Rice, *A–Z of Wellbeing* (Milton Keynes: Authentic, 2022), p. 77.

A-Z of Wellbeing for Children

Lots of ways to look after your mental health

Ruth Rice and Debbie Green

Looking after our wellbeing inside and out is really important.

A–Z of Wellbeing for Children provides simple things for kids aged 7 to 11 to do and think about that will help them work out how to look after themselves better.

Ruth Rice and Debbie Green show children that Jesus is the very best teacher when it comes to wellbeing as they explore the Five Ways to Wellbeing: Connecting, Learning, Getting Active, Taking Notice and Giving. Each of the 26 words of wellbeing are accompanied by stories about Jesus to read, ideas to try, pictures to colour and prayers to pray. The activities are designed for a young person to do either on their own, with a friend or an adult who cares for them.

A–Z of Wellbeing for Children encourages kids to be who God made them to be and provides them with tools that can help them look after their mental health.

Ideal for children to use as a personal workbook alongside *A-Z of Wellbeing Toolkit* teaching sessions.

978-1-78893-397-1

We trust you enjoyed reading this book from Authentic. If you want to be informed of any new titles from this author and other releases you can sign up to the Authentic newsletter by scanning below:

Online:
authenticmedia.co.uk

Follow us:

www.ingramcontent.com/pod-product-compliance
Lightning Source LLC
Chambersburg PA
CBHW080857090426
42735CB00014B/3174